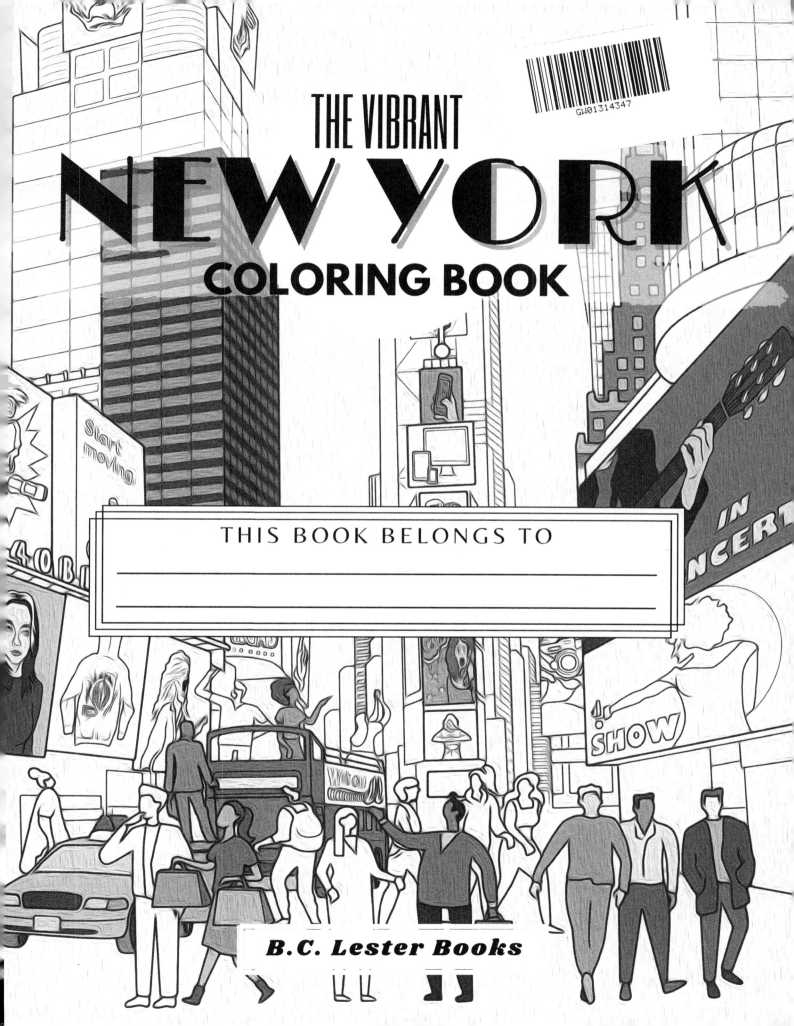

A MESSAGE FROM THE PUBLISHER

Hey, thank you for making the purchase, we really hope you enjoy this book. If you have the chance, then all feedback is greatly appreciated. We have put a lot of effort into making this book, so if you are not completely satisfied, please email us at ben@bclesterbooks.com and we will do our best to address any issues. If you have any suggestions, enquries or want to send us a selfie with this book, then email at the same address - ben@bclesterbooks.com

Is this book misprinted? Send us an email at ben@bclesterbooks.com with a photo of the misprint and we will send out another copy!

IF YOU ENJOYED THIS COLORING EXPERIENCE, THEN YOU MAY LIKE:

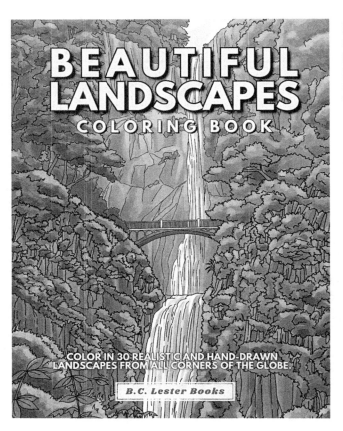

ISBN-10: 1913668401

Unwind, relax, and bring some of our planet's most beautiful natural scenery to life with color!

Before You Start

Test your coloring equipment here for bleedthrough. This book has been designed for use with coloring pencils. This coloring book is NOT recommended for paint, pastel or highlighters...

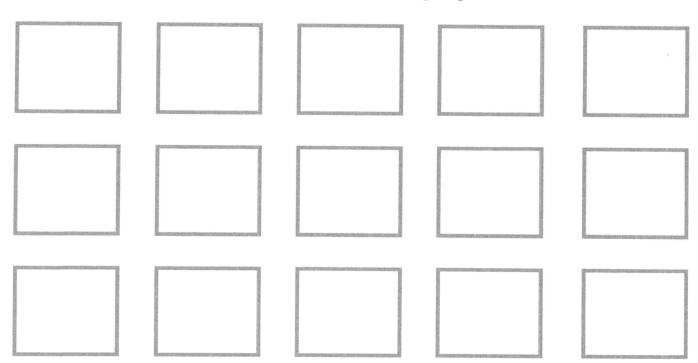

Visit us at www.bclesterbooks.com for more!

No part of this book may be copied, reproduced or sold without the express permission from the copyright owner.

Copyright B.C. Lester Books 2021. All rights reserved.

Ready To Start?
Relax, unwind, and enjoy the experience!

B.C. Lester Books

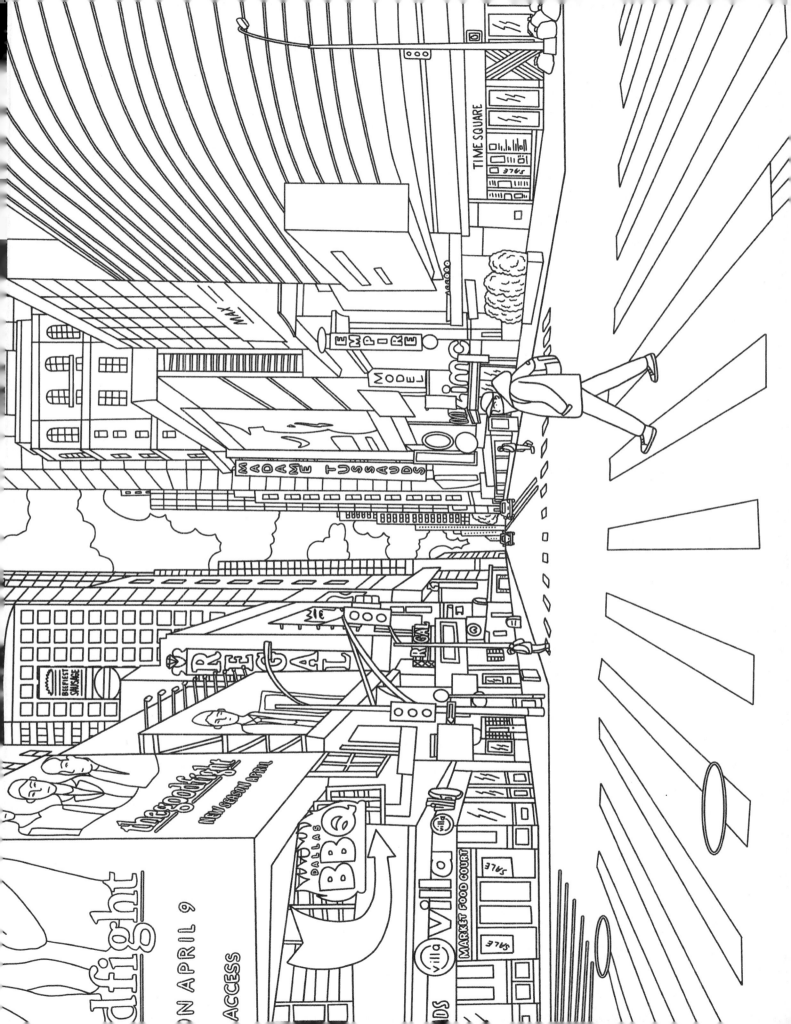

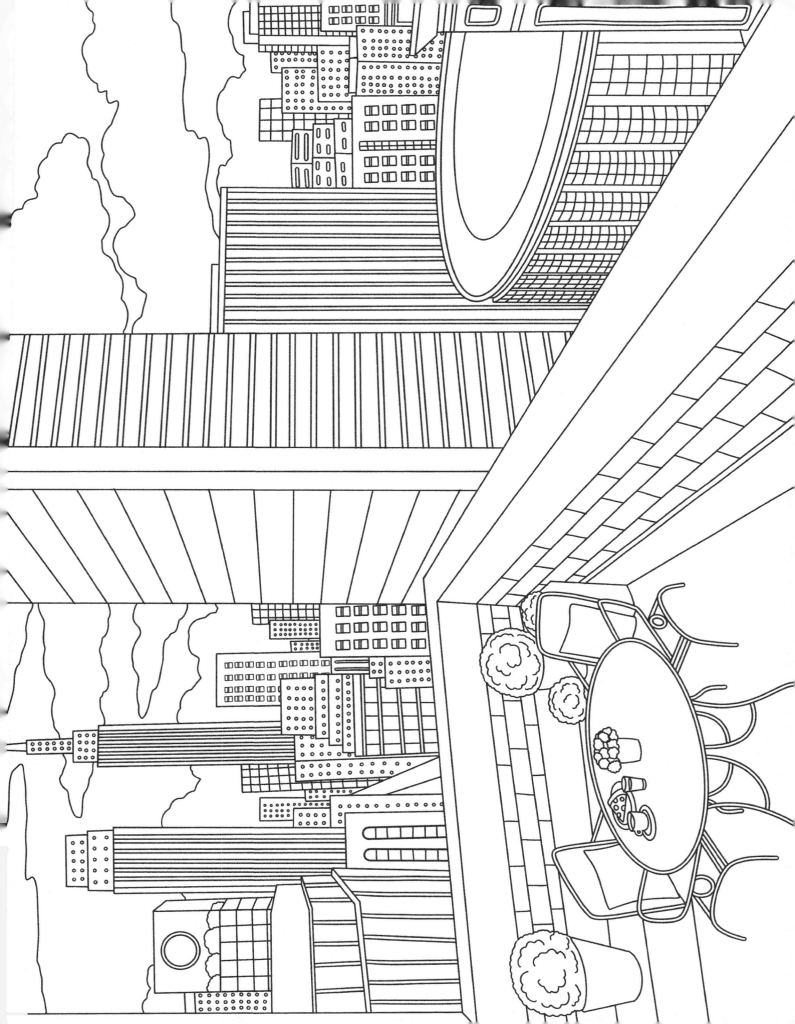

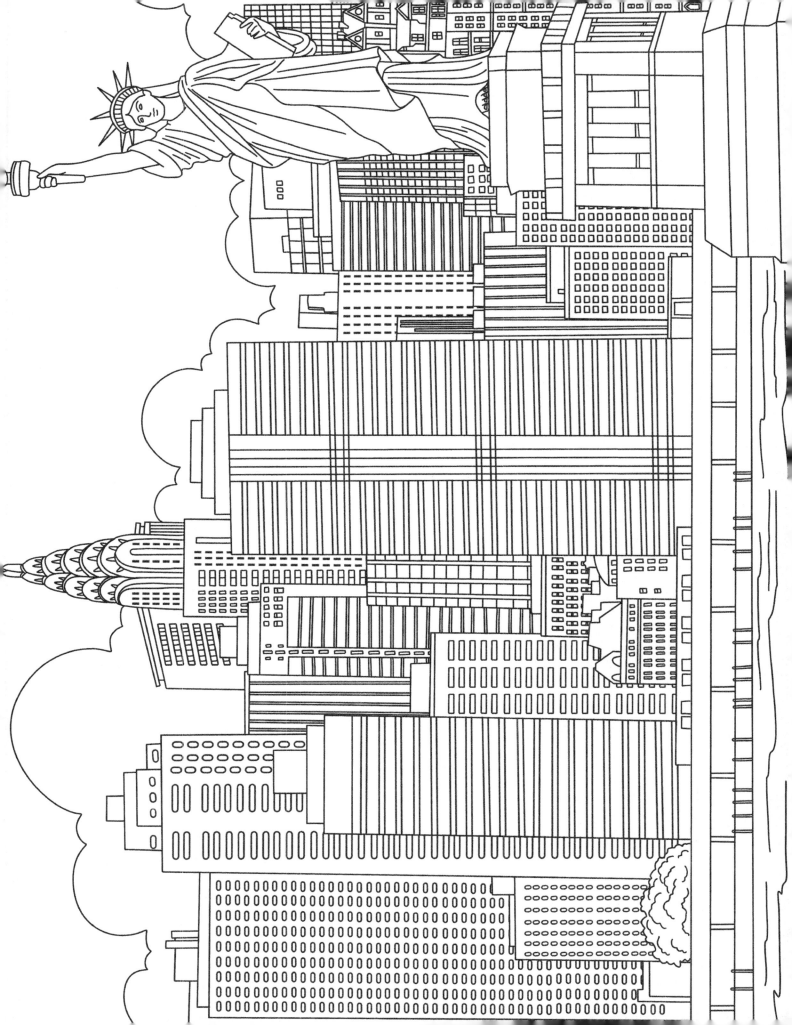

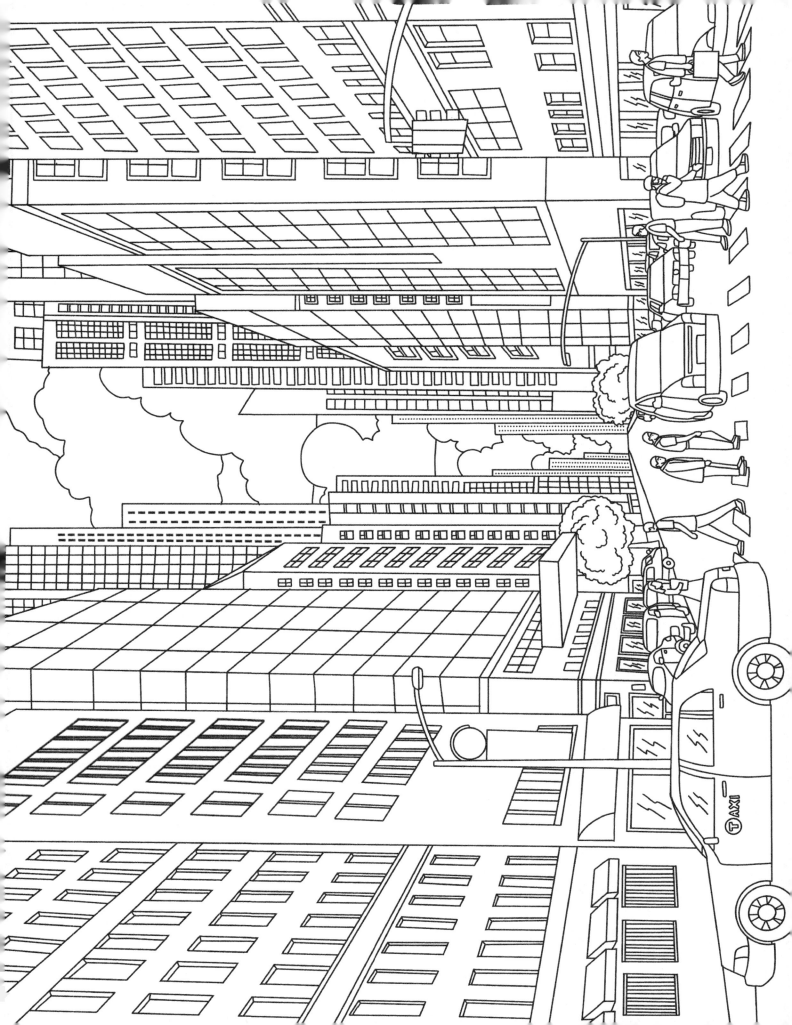

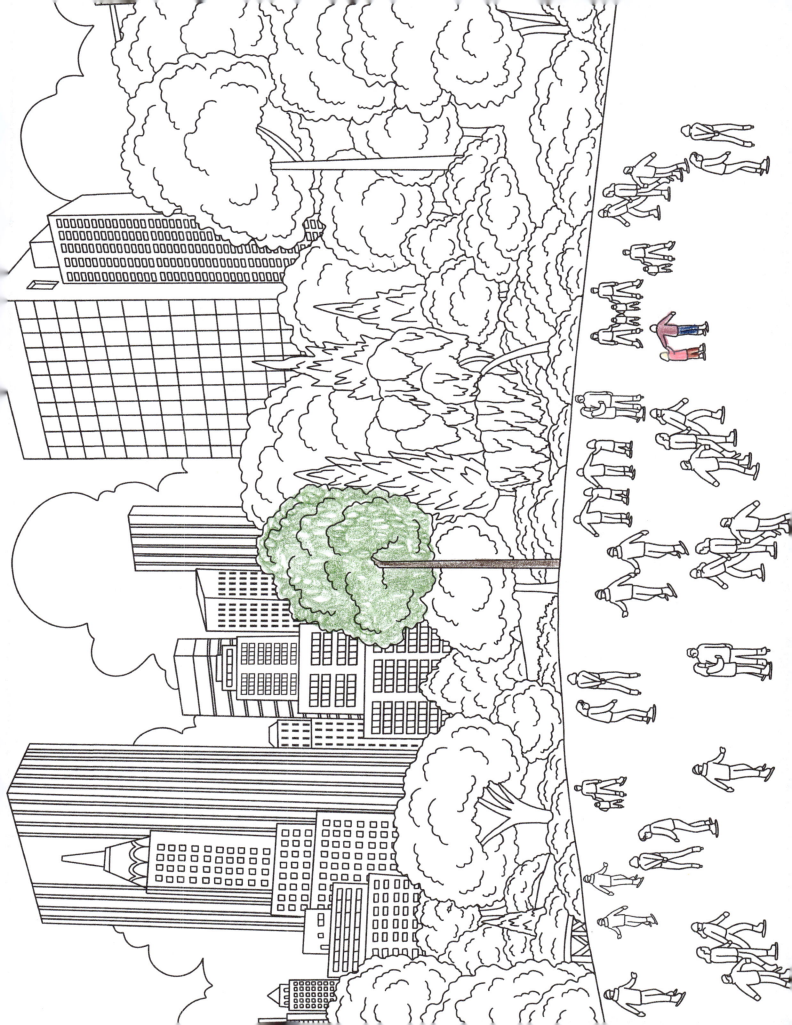

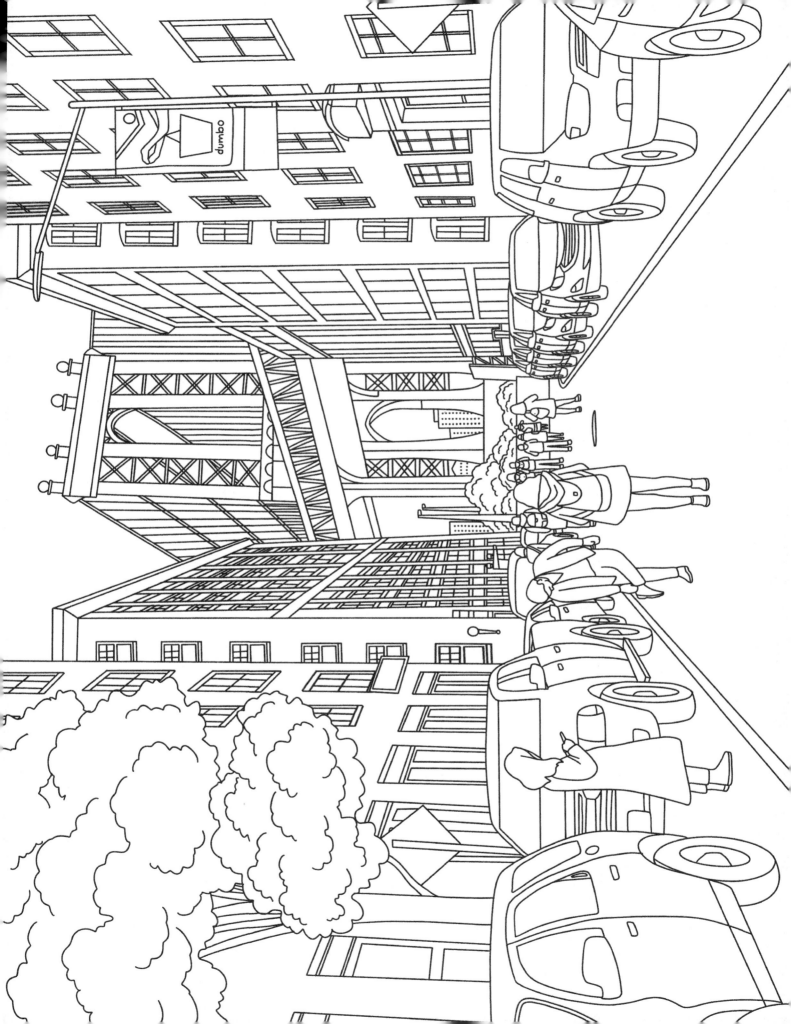

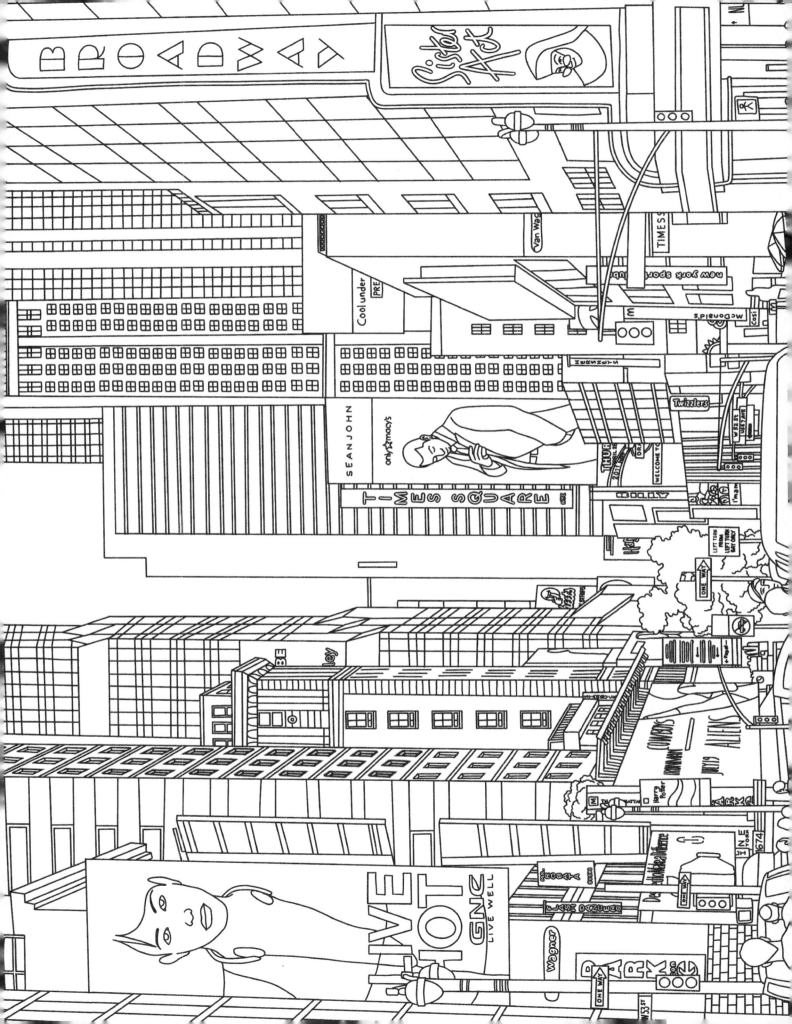

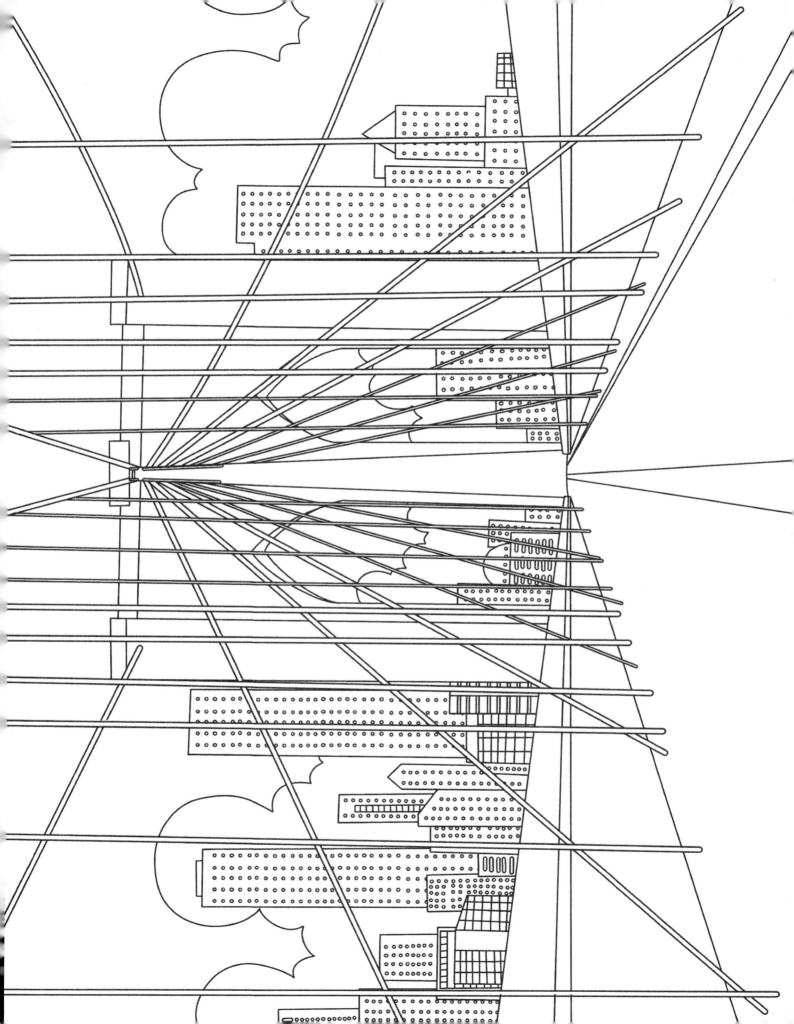

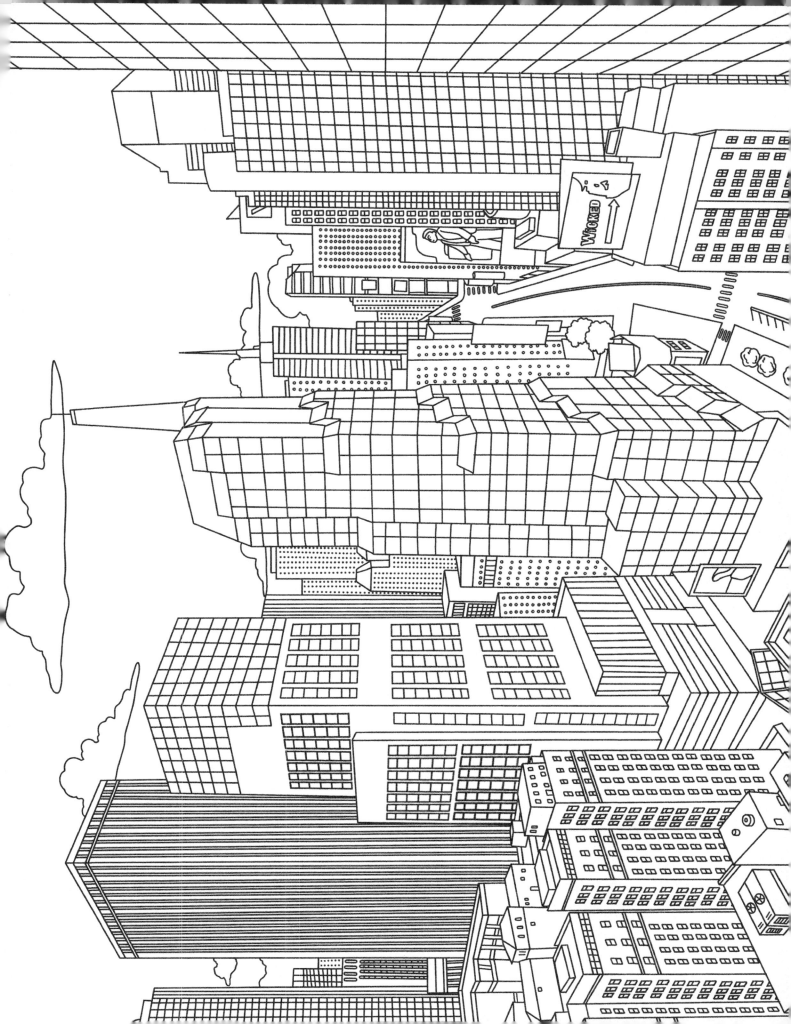

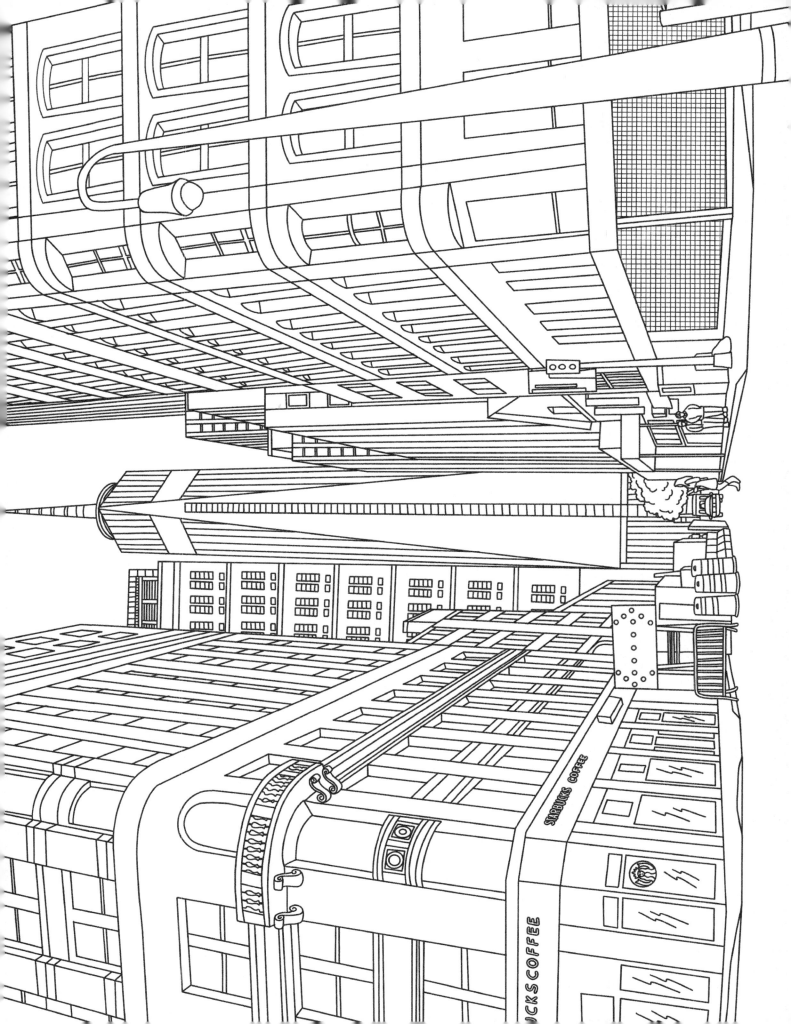

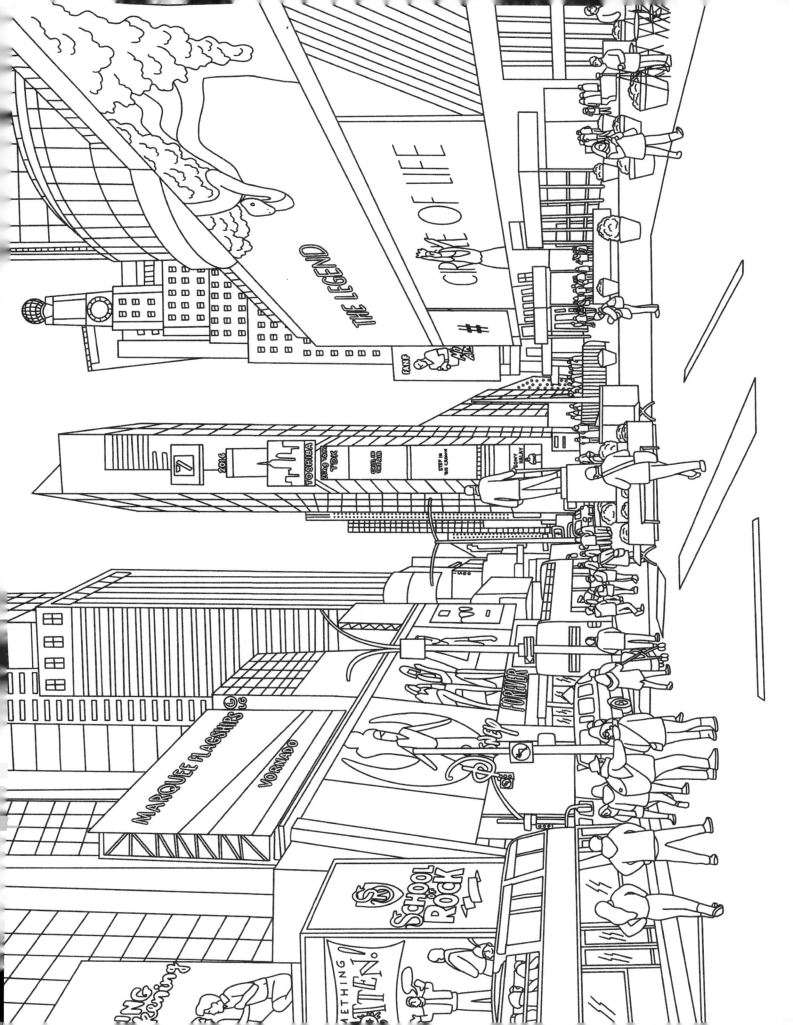

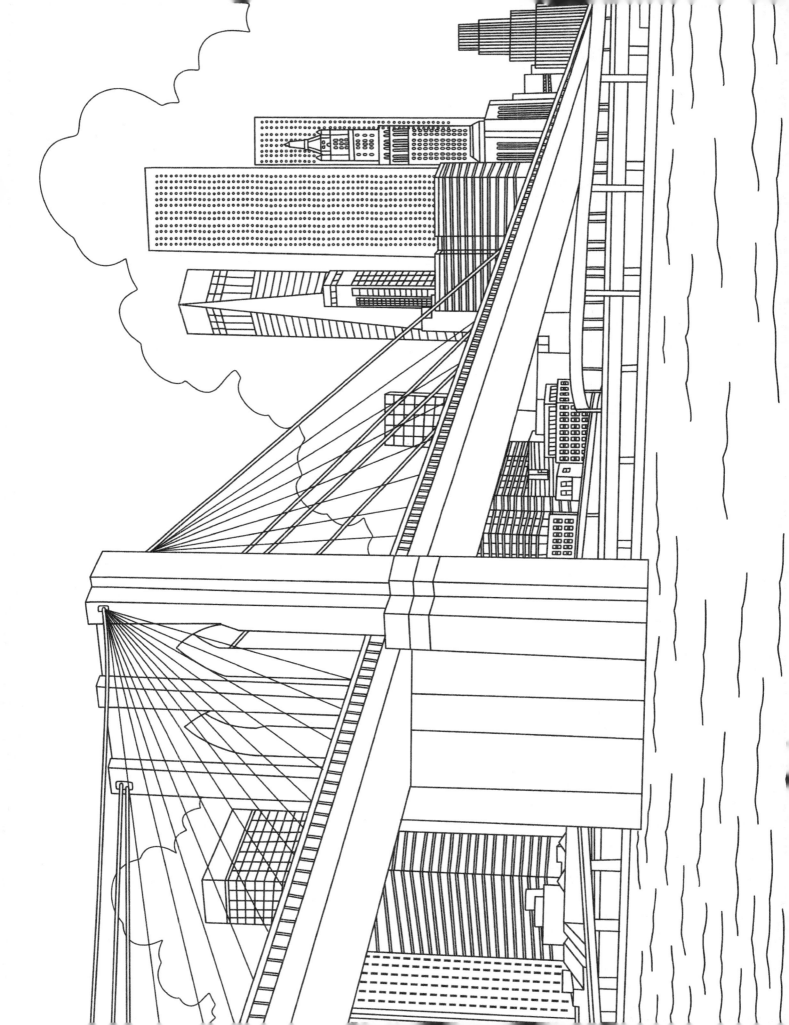

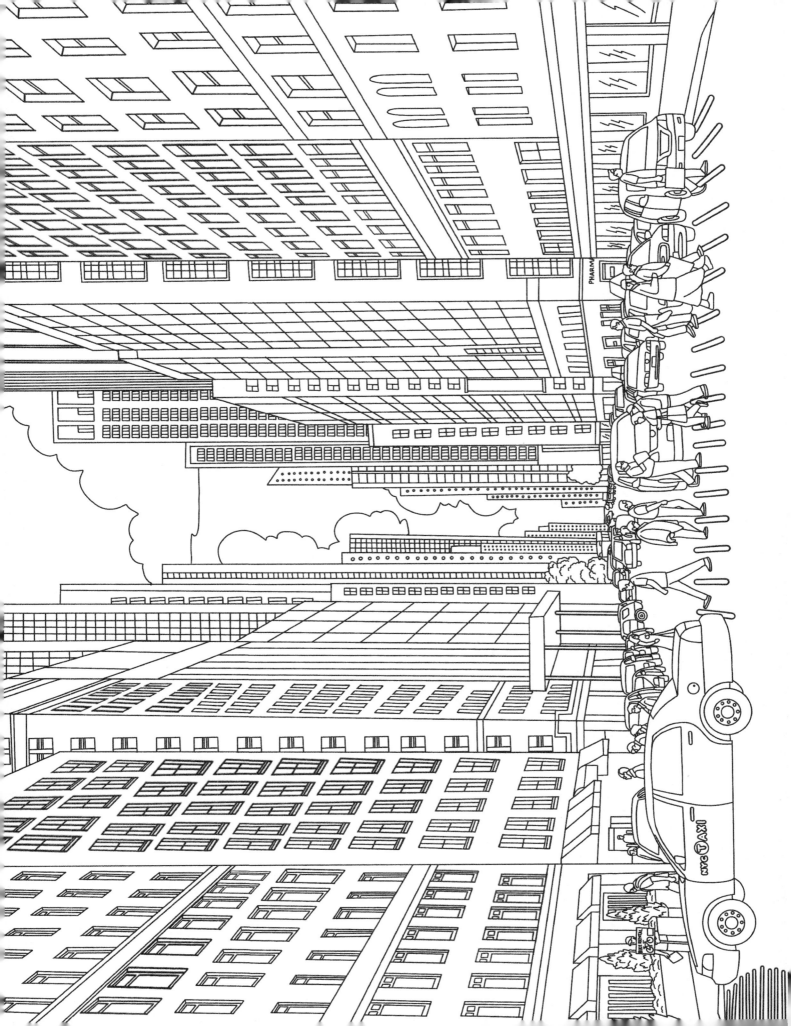

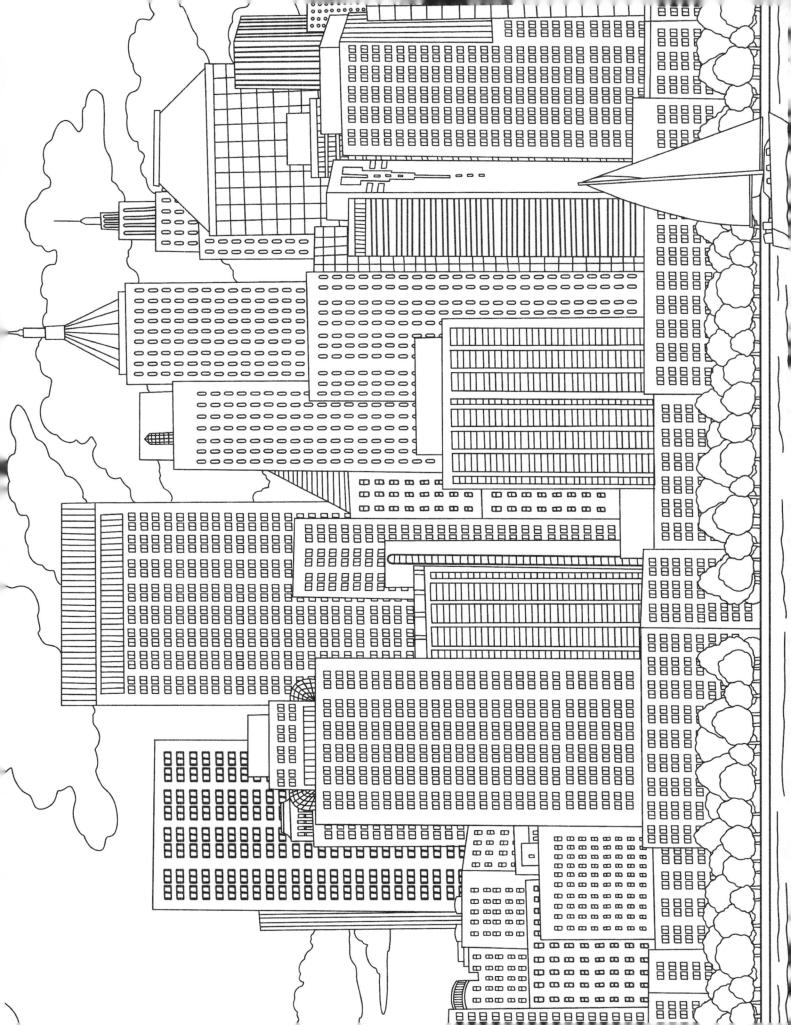

Printed in Great Britain
by Amazon